THE RAMIFICATIONS

THE RAMIFICATIONS

JOHN ZEDOLIK

RESOURCE *Publications* • Eugene, Oregon

THE RAMIFICATIONS

Copyright © 2024 John Zedolik. All rights reserved. Except for brief quotations in critical publications or reviews, no part of this book may be reproduced in any manner without prior written permission from the publisher. Write: Permissions, Wipf and Stock Publishers, 199 W. 8th Ave., Suite 3, Eugene, OR 97401.

Resource Publications
An Imprint of Wipf and Stock Publishers
199 W. 8th Ave., Suite 3
Eugene, OR 97401

www.wipfandstock.com

PAPERBACK ISBN: 979-8-3852-1856-1
HARDCOVER ISBN: 979-8-3852-1857-8
EBOOK ISBN: 979-8-3852-1858-5

New American Bible, World Bible Publishers, Inc. ©*1970*

The Greek New Testament, United Bible Societies ©*1983*

Table of Contents

Alternative Route 4
Heliosebas. 11
Prestidigation 24
La Fiamma Invisibile 29
Twenty-Four in Twenty-Four. 34

Acknowledgments

"Alternative Route," in *Lost Lake Folk Opera*, V. 8, n. 1, "Waterways" Issue, Autumn 2023, Winona, MN (Autumn 2023)

Alternative Route

    i.   *water waylaid*

Used to stand at the mountain's base
a monument to Joe Palooka until some

cretins stole the bas-relief of the comic-strip
boxer's profile to replace with the dull

graffiti of obscenity upon the indistinct
shades and hues of weathered concrete—

    But turn right, nevertheless, through

the gap and pass the spring that used to splash
innocently and freely over just gray rocks

and emerald moss until stolen by some bottling
company that has hidden the cool source

within ridged metal walls and under boxing roof,
so locked with the icy key of commerce

    until we reach the crooked T aside
    the run whose murmur and wrinkle

    we must imagine from the slope
    and the unceasing wheels that drive this trip

      ii.   *in memoriam ad . . .?*

We never turned right onto the bridge,
and I still have no experience of it

and now only the bare knowledge
of maps, for gramma and grampa's

house lay on the mountain's flank,
which dropped, splayed, after the summit

to the left, which climbed past the small
sandstone memorial, pink and worn

like a well-used pencil eraser, to a portion
of Major-General Sullivan's march to destroy

the loyalists and the Iroquois beyond
the northern border in New York State—

burn their villages and crops—just a genocide
for the latter in that looming winter

upon the plateau and beside the lakes—

> which you might miss—as you ascend
> to the lip and now descend to all that is below

iii.   solid focus

Near the road, in the woods
running down lay a millstone

to which we would lope,
on occasion, after leaving

the car and gather around at least
once for a photo—the great wheel

quartz-flecked, adamant omphalos
of this tight world, even discarded,

at an angle upon the bedrock's
wrinkled slope over which the quiet

leaves would close again—the millstone
never around our necks—as we were

young, nimble

                so scrambled back up
                to the ribbon leading us down—

with new (or renewed) knowledge
of the old ways and their discarded wares

iv.   *partial reconstruction*

The folly stood a shell of cinder
blocks unconcerned in those materials

parvenu—with white stone—or probably
plaster—statues *contrapposto* curving

in the half-dozen niches that scooped out
the façade on the ledge of authentic rock—

and paused incomplete—for the drivers
to pass judgment upon caprice, pride,

and short-sighted desire to reproduce
Europe overlooking this valley that lights

its eyes upon that center of river running
to estuary then ocean in wet miles a hundred

and a half, counted by no drop swallowed
in the streams, unlike beads as we, hoping

for memory, a rudder in the swells
through awful eternity

> v. *surface tension*

Devil's elbow curved above
and around the fires burning—

still—underground—a hellish
scene, to be sure, if one could find

a golden bough among the aspens
and descend like Aeneas at the Sybil's

advice, but no such guide was discovered
or wanted by us as we only needed

the surface and a safe measure of speed
through that sheer bend to the slack end

of little thrill, where the houses soon
sprouted again, a spring of safety after

the chill of sharp angle that stirred
the gut and certified life

      vi.   *leavening*

Saint John the Baptist Church sits,
modest and quieter than the Evangelist

who has been generous with his name,
within which gramma's remains will lie

    in a future summer

boxed for her last mass, at this point
where the route regularizes to city street

and no smoke rises except at times
escaping the usual ovens and stoves—

and their over-cooked meals—so on down
to the nadir of the river that would quench

all if it could roll uphill and reach
the dry summit that only knows wet

from rain, which sinks into the soil,
someday reaching that river so far below

this road whose serpent-twistings
call for caution but lash the senses

and mind to reel in the thread
whose ends are farther asunder

than the artic pole and its opposition

vii.   porous depths

So after short time, again

rubber grips the road—back up and over
to remember the passed ruins,

the marks of what was, what remains,
to fix upon you like nitrogen

upon root nodes underground
nourishing but perhaps forgotten

or even unknown as you twist
and turn through ways that require

skill and clear sight until you loop
under and wait, unconcerned,

for falling water that always trickles
through channels left by careless earth

to insist, to find what is left
of all below and behind.

Heliosebas

The door in the tomb
of some un-famous French citizen,
led to wall within the confines
of *Le Cimitière Pere Lachaise*

so led only back out into the hard
garden and its attendant maze
where old trees raised shades
conjured only from the sun

whose purview found its limit
at the carved seraphim and crosses
below which and beyond the rays,
the dwellers must seek another one.

*

Out on the Boulevard de Ménilmontant
there must be *un bureau de tabac.*
I do not smoke, for the billows would cloud

my vision, but I would like to know my memory
is sound though the mind's misplacement
of a small shop among thousands would not mean

my faculties sense through a haze like that upon
the near air of those who do exhale the nicotine fumes,
Yet I like my own maps to align with those outside

*

But if blind—

which we may be despite our sight
so desire equipment to sound the depths
that plummet out of our faculty's grasps

as if no depth at all, just a flat world,
a slate slab, and nothing, everything only
slate until the cosmos ends in its own wall.

*

but back to the bones, which do inhabit
the skin, which we do sense, as we plumb
the other person who stands opposite,
our senses knives whose edges and points
gleam our desire to carve down without
cutting and calling the needed blood out

where it would die

*

but how akin to the ribs of a great bridge,
say the Golden Gate as it glides across the bay
to Sausalito and back—just steel only shedding

the rain that will fall into the writhing sea below
or ascend upon vaporization unto the sky
above the colossus whose feet sink into the lightless

depths where no chance of a wound from the sun's
arrows makes for a sealed system of impermeable
skin, impervious to influences above, its own

country, no ecstasy à la Saint Theresa of Ávila,
Bernini stone-skill or not,
        for which desire,

"*. . . cuperem ipse graves tum rumpere terras.*"[1]

*

1. "Then I, myself, would burst the heavy earth."
(The ghost of Cretheus, Jason's grandfather, to his son Aeson and wife, Alcimede)
—Valerius Flaccus, *Argonautica*, Book 1, line 746 (translation mine)

Regardless,

> the transfer is to others' minds, hands,
>
> which may be the result of the inhumation,
> inhumanization, no chthonic deity
> are we
>
> so minds
> stretching through the soil, upward-seeking roots to
> burst onto the sky as green shoots
>
> to the sun and sibling stars partaking of this nectar of the
> ever-living

NO, not for us are these strong liquors to keep ourselves aware of ourselves, one-to-one,

adhesive strip to backing—none of that obliterating in-between, the molecules like microbes infecting with oblivion ourselves-ourselves

*

Empress Theodora told the fleeing, fearful Emperor Justinian that it would be better to die in the purple than live without that distinction,

and so purple is the color of the prideful sun

that covers the wearer, the bearer of its light when under its aegis, a burden of unfeather,

only considered when it is waning, which then becomes heavy as the only time remaining

*

A twist of bone and feather
and, if skin there, surely leather

the coat of the once-bird
protection now so absurd

under such raw elements
without the needed sentiments

that would feel the ice and fire
sweat or shiver, in dire

circumstance if lacking the integument
now shriveled in abasement

a shred of its erstwhile integrity
that might now summon reasoned pity

if its bearer sensed any hurt,
which in time does, with mercy, desert.

*

G: "So, no DESSERT for you not because you don't DESERVE but because sweets are no concern of yours at this point (of no point).
H: "I understand; it is not cruelty that drives this refusal, only a desire, a responsibility to tell the truth.
G: "I am happy we are in agreement."
H: "Certainly, since taste is only temporary." (*H dissolves with a neutral expression into what must be all.*)
G: "Amen"

*

The hole has ragged edges as if gnawed by long-gone rodents
and said edges now giving themselves in powder to the wind
who is only passing through like an old-time salesman
though with a less fancy, tawdry suit since none is necessary

if you are said wind who needs not market himself
any sartorial seams since to be ONLY current

but pressed with this desire to be permanent "facts"
so selfish and yearning to ape the seasons and vegetal
growth—if only green we were—even sere and withered
in winter—better than red blood that will not spiral
through millennia like sequoias that ONLY bend that wind

*

*Dante morì di malaria perchè paludi sono
inevitabili quindi dovremmo goderci
la commedia mortale*

che muore troppo presto.[2]

*

No apotropaic
      for the root of the elegiac
But we scribble and scratch
      the eventual winner to match
My fingers at the effort cramp
      even before I must decamp

. . . επειδη δηλα τα ιχνη, ω ανθροποι, μη μέλλετε φευγειν τους κινδυνους.[3]

*

Yet in the meantime I shall observe it,
although it all, leaf and stone, is fleeting
and I do not desire to be bleating

2. Dante died of malaria because swamps
are inevitable, so we must enjoy
the mortal comedy

that dies too soon. (words and translation mine)

3. "Since the footsteps are clear, men, do not hesitate to flee the danger."

—Aesop, Fable 147 (translation mine)

even an old man, ancient as Sanskrit
or some needy and lead-headed nitwit
for whom comfort is always retreating
beyond the point of earth and sky meeting
regardless if enough is just surfeit
I will cleave in this particular earth
whose stuff will crumble darkly in my hand
hold its water until the winds arise
to leave us little here but hollow dearth
that feels to the frail senses worse than bland
but after I have maintained my surmise.

*

Tithonus senex non suam vitam aestimavit quia factus est gryllus
Sed ego cantem usquam, fovens calorem alarum mearum[4]

*

Acne blooms in pain and scarlet on my face like offered flowers to the war god,
        which might even bleed if
spawned from a hellish enough nursery, my anxiety, my fear
        that breeds in its hothouse atmosphere
these eruptions, this face of angry Mars, Deimos and Phobos unnecessary,
        his emblem, a wolf to my comfort
though claws that impress a life's sensation may be welcome to those uncertain
        of life and its necessary feelings

*

Like those—
who nod too much under poppy's sway, the lotus-eaters
whom Odysseus met on the way back to Penelope
and his husband life, and many don't have
the secret sauce to stay around
intact above the ground

---

4. Tithonus did not value his own life since he became a cricket,
I would sing anyway, cherishing the heat of my wings (words and translation mine)

    so

. . . hasteth yow; the sonne wole adoun;[5]

*

Yet when I extend the finger or the pen
I feel I can write the life forever

forfend the utter end, as if the noting
of a working spider, spotted and spindly,
upon his near-invisible trap between
the hostas, lush in this spring, lines
secured on the leaves and stair railings
of our deck, bouncing upon a sudden

breeze not so strong to detach the hunter
from its comfort, means, and moor

will guarantee no surcease from sense
or—at least—detach the pain and fear

with strokes ending/continuing in ink
or electronic pixels black as the—

*

An ex-colleague said she happened to be sitting   (This was an honor for her.)
by chance in 1993 on a flight back from San Francisco
with Alan Ginsberg, who asked her to hold his
hand due to his fear, which she dutifully did,
while both survived the untethered life—   (though this IS the life!)

but Ginsberg did not '97
even with feet on the mother ground   (but no excerpt will he get)

*

---

5. Geoffrey Chaucer: words of the host, Harry Bailey, to the Parson, the *Parson's Prologue*, l. 70, the *Canterbury Tales*

The heat dulls the air as age, old metal
so slows the progress of our steps
and strips desire of its claws

since the atmosphere is just cotton,
cotton lying leadly on us these days
of extreme-late spring that will lead

only into hot summer further deadening
the nerves under the questionable
aegis of a hazed sun who might hope
to shine with few heavy veils
to the thirsty down here where

sweat takes away our water
to settle on the competing earth
leaving us deserts, who have

sought *Sol* on innumerable occasions,
but the tilt of the axis makes
the globe fickle, a constant
inconstant, whom we only know
will return to the previous old
wobbles at last leaving us

spun off, still, and quiet, behind

*

metem(psychotic) desires   in which we dwelled but really apart
  make us many times   if one believes the lore and dogma
    what awaits in the word like the comfort of the womb

Psyche, the soul, the ancients thought   that cradled us in the inception
  a butterfly to flit out of the *soma* of what we wish would be forever
    when the flesh falters the last that taking of res(spir)ation, breath

*

Spiritvs profanvs
which we contain and exchange
can only take us so far

as the heart beats—a billion perhaps—
inhalation and exhalation
over the inverted trees of the lung

whose roots lead upward to
the mouth that drinks in the light
provided by the finite days

and

*

Afflatus down down manna parakletos
      not parakeet us parrot us we poor grounders
           but something some sustenance *neo novus*
                not just a bone—are we dogs?—to gnaw the time
No, breathe unto us thine flame *Parens Noster*,
      unhallowed be our game though we doggedly
           pursue the goal on hard court, grass field, or pitch
                so we look for that extra boost, that mojo for the win

*

Saints abjectified, mortified, homicide
to reach that light they believe transcends the sun
whose rays transfix the Hagia like Bernini's rays
in the Cornaro chapel in Santa Maria Della Vittoria

in Rome, not far from the Fountain of the Naiads
who frolic in their own low, liquid pleasure,
perhaps a balance for the piercing sublime
of her in the baroque of marble folds whose eyes

pupil-lacking must be equipped for the spectrum
of the divine, far beyond red or indigo and even infrared
or ultraviolet, but we of flesh have no such blanks

so are blinded even by our *Sol* through the ninety-three

million miles of emptiness between us and that source
of all life, which Akhenaton deemed the chief god,
and so, why not?—in the desert—in the millennia
ago whose brethren will stretch after us into their
own kind of deserts with who knows whom to
describe their awful silence that provide simulacra
to our eventual condition under sand or moist
soil whose substance is too thick for thinking.

*

    (But I drive my dreams like a team of oxen
    (Cannot flesh toughen to stronger metal?)

    But the Colossus of Rhodes collapsed and his sections carted away
    to be melted into new Hellenistic delights that might even now be
    seen but unrecognized—so changed—does the Wonder still exist?

    might ask the philosophers of ontology and such concerns of identity
    solid to molten to solid again in a new wrinkle, twist, bearing
    the identical molecules—just a physical change—so can reverse

    and raise up the representation of Helios guarding the harbor, under
    his aegis but of χαλκός in a renewed state and epoch, legs on each pier
    or not, metempsychosis for the soulless, hollow strider, but what for us?

*

An uncle lost at sea, off Block Island, Rhode Island,
has a cenotaph somewhere, as all found of the small
craft of November was the screen door to the cabin
so no earth will shield his substance from the sun

these thirty years and some so offer a different
sort of transformation (where perhaps

        his bones are dreams made
        those are children the pearls of his eyes
        nothing of him fades
        but suffers a sea change
        into memory and paintings on the paneled wall)[6]

        than that offered by the box

of wood and its surrounding glove of soil so snugly
fitting to the polish that must wear despite its showroom sheen

as all do except those airy spirits who bathe only
in the streams of the sky's ocean and sun's shower

*

        Is to go beyond, still to be?
        in the dark, can we sense?
        will there be recompense?
        if in that soundless sea
        is it a matter of desert?
        a sempiternal justice?
        beyond this brief interstice?
        or a return to matter inert

*

—perhaps we are only oneiric
images fired by the charges

between God's synapses
so should not worry

about independent existence,
not to drive the point into the ground

that is already waiting to receive us
no need to over-satiate
that greedy gullet,
down and dark

    6. inspired by William Shakespeare, Ariel's song, *The Tempest*, I.ii. 398-402

*
                                                                                           rises

Already passed is the solstice, though as the heat
the light
                lessens

so teaches us sometime unwilling acolytes
the lesson of life

our perception of paradox makes
only sense to us—with our thirsty sensibility

*

Orpheus on the path back,
cobbles worn just about

to dark glass by those downward

and you going up

        (Did your feet sense the tread
          against the stone's still remaining grain?)

and so your eyes as well
for a time until

impatience and insecurity
drew them back like the entirety of the others

for Eurydice
who was there
wouldn't depart

        (No danger of Hades reneging on his word;
         your playing was that good.)

but your gut churned
and your eyes turned

> (no Medusa there to petrify your form)

to her—and the bridge broke—

down she retreated
like a pebble dropped from the heights
without a ping and echo
but, hey, your legs take you to the top

a resurrection of one

not enough

but for your doubt, it must suffice.

Now keep your squinting eyes—

unused to the sun—

only upon the green
—the living tissue—

yours for not even a song.

> and anyhow, if we only pursue the sun
> at a cool and logical angle—
> silence the instinct spike and emotional jangle
> only at a salubrious walk and not break-ankle run—
>
> no reason at all to come undone,
> like a mind disconsolate,
> savor time's salt,

*

But earthly desire has no reasonable god

Prestidigitation

1.

My odor of naivety drew the pork-pie-hat man
with his matching suit of black and off-yellow check
to my seat on the El train after he had worked
his three-shell game and dispensed
a lucky twenty bucks in one crackling bill

Or maybe it was just my attention to the gamble

but he laid his cards out, asked twenty down
to double my money if I found the marble
under its carapace like a treasured hermit crab
so I followed his hands and those three helmets
sliding on the well-sat plastic of the empty seat

next to mine, thought I knew where the jewel
was hiding, reached into my pocket (front, at least!)
to bring Andrew Jackson to the light when
one of Chicago's finest burst into the car
then ran after the man—and the woman who had supposedly

won twenty dollars—but an accomplice, of course—

so I learned with the aid of law enforcement but would
probably have lost on my own, too poor and innocent
to leave temptation to other credulous hands

2.

The sea wrack and miscellany—thick brown carapaces
of the horseshoe crabs—and their spent egg sacs
like a mess of old keys on a string

common shells and tossed-up, dead fish with dried,
fractional eye up to the sky in apparent wonder

attract the attention of the beachcomber who deems
the detritus gems of the sea and marvels at its generosity
up and down the length of the high-tide line, whose
deposits are a ghost of the salt-foam wave, scalloped
at its termination like those mollusks of the same name

but are these pieces, trinkets, jetsam, decayers
gold even as they glisten under the continent-limit's
sky or just grit to be left and ground by the next
wave's billowing blade, held in salty hand of protean
predisposition not averse to pummel any beach or strand

by their nature—faces fertile for a slap of Selene's tug—
so rough already under the tons of cracked cartilage
and ceaseless churning of brine and her quartz allies,
tiny though patient and mighty that will polish all
to a smooth surface appropriate for such as the sea?

3.

Appearance is only skin, a rind thin
over unseen flesh plunging to core
that resists all efforts of our steel bore
to retrieve a sample of truth therein
the time that we squander when we begin
is much more fruitfully used to explore
why our eyes are so eager to adore
that which is only fog, empty within
Perhaps seeing all is too much and so
we seek the shielding glare of surface sheen
much comfort in the dazzle blinding out
the light of what lies beyond—is, has been
those subtle strong phantoms thus apropos
for this lifelong task threatening a rout

4.

Cogito ergo dvbio
        so cherish the certainty in that welter
Evito modum subivnctivvm
        Stay in the indicative lane

5.

"Do not interpretations belong to God?"[7]

asked Joseph to those asking

        but if a Greek would have known
those dreams—CERTAIN—ascended to the uncertain
world of waking through the gates of horn
instead of ivory, mere fluff

        nothing to worry about

if one is gifted enough by God to discern
prophecy from fantasy

that guilds most eyes
that peep "as through a glass darkly"[8]

6.

And my own wonder continues
whether regarding liquid or airy
mundane or faërie
the contents of any vision, any
sighting—any content at all?
that would direct my limbs
after some considered decision

    7. fr. Genesis 40:8
    8. I Corinthians 13:12

I would take even the lesser light of the sometimes
guide of the night—crane my neck
up with high vertebrae torsion to seek
that which down here I will not find

7.

As children, we played in summer well into the twilight
        among the scent of dew and grass, some of which had ingrained themselves
upon our knees, palms, and souls,

        until mothers, sensing that real night was imminent,
shouted across the lawns and strips of forest that gave way to just
        trees on the other side of the creek beyond which lay the west

where the sun had disappeared long ago to take the journey into the dark
        underworld where lay jackals in wait to devour the bright, hot
delicacy of the depthless disk so steal light from every curve of earth
        the solar blood just flesh in the black gullets of those snappers whose
teeth glisten just below the upper rim of spreading dark we push back without
        a thought in sympathy of the traveler that must (we determine) return to us

who will always be children gathering the last fluffs of light that linger
        into the false fire of day we decree for our eternal play
since, as children, we have only to deem and it will be

8.

A: "I see nothing but a dun expanse."

B: "Your eyes are blind."

A: "Blind to all that is false"

B: "So starved of necessary sustenance"

A: "I feed off the fruits of *no thing*."

B: "And how does that taste?"

9.

Sleight of hand is slight(ly) off hand
just *modvs operandi*—quotidian,
even if it paints the day and sky viridian,
at my unthinking, so easy request

nonchalance is good for one's health
wards off senescence while encouraging virulence
even as the years climb Babel-high in their obstinance
displaying each step higher with a flourish

like a flag repeatedly planted in small conquest
through grade after sweating grade in profusion
brings the climber only the comfort of illusion
with which to enrobe the so sensitive I/eye

10.

Through travails, we keep a face to the cynosure
and gaze through the veil/vale whose lengths
carry distance into dimness and disappear

but the unseen is perhaps better than a screen
whose filter may be faulty so let in the not-so-
certainly-wanted light in which may shine

("Then the veil of the temple was torn down the middle."⁹)

the truth   ἡ αλήθεια   *veritas*
that just burns eyes to clear sight
unasked for by rod cone nerve and mind

---

9. Luke 23:45

La Fiamma Invisibile

1.

So with quick violence and, for good measure, the past perfect tense,
one's last words sometimes vanish into ash, or, had vanished

So already past, shut from now and hence into the consuming heat
of transformation as go those most cherished elements

despite the benefit they would offer if saved from willed
immolation, a sacrifice to spleen or the cousin pride

better if no one gains than if one does and one does not, so
a dog in the manger you, wishes none to gain, naught for all,

in a fit of desperate pique, which we should avoid
if we can, just another fire for someone to put out

2.

I always choose wisely what to keep and what to jettison,
while leaving Chicago, a *Blues Brothers* poster stood, a large
stiff-backed hand and still "goodbye," from the Dumpster

in the apartment building's back lot, as did the Ikea desk
of many drawers that I had assembled myself seven years
back and seven hundred miles east but no honor for my labors

or its durability as we pulled away from the gate in haste
to never look back at least in twenty and more years
and whatever changes rose and sunk beside the inland sea

whose jade waters could not hold me, so away, away, I cast
into my greater ocean of memory where the mineral cast
may preserve its opalescence even as time works all to deliquescence

3.

So pull pull pull the rankling thread that cranes, a claw into inconvenient space
until
        you have no more warp and weft only the helical chaos—a bird's nest—
        of matter
perfection will often lead to dissolution since the integrity of your textile resides
        in the unraveling that accompanies the living wear of those pliant
        materials
that cloak you in soft fibers that will not last for a future archaeologist's look
        just scattered dust, if that, swirled back into the cosmos, raw cotton
        waiting
for another combination—just right—to craft consciousness—a new goddess
from the froth
        of sidereal sea that provides another nest for chance to work its sorcery
wrapped in new weeds, a new guise, which broadcasts control and certainty, but
yet cloaks,
        hides the fate that might whirl this new design to shreds wanting any
        angle

4.

Cast off tears should be enough
no *taurobolium* necessary and subsequent
bathing in said bull's blood

for symbolic resurrection
in this new life after the grief
that knocks shut the old, a thick

door of iron, throw away the key
into the same rocky creek that pushes
its water, its sediments, and critter

remains to the ocean, who will use
all such detritus for building its bed
and nourishing its next creatures

whose sense of self may have to wait
millions of years to just the average
"I am I"—another from the rest

5.

Ἐν αρκη ην ὁ λόγος, και ὁ λόγος ην προς τον θεόν, και θεος ην ὁ λόγος.[10]

—but we were never with the word just castoffs, only creatures, permanently passive despite our actions.

We are only those spun into action. After all, substance begins with *sub*—
under or secondary—
and we are just both.
Perhaps rising after sloughing off the dross prefix—so not fixed any more to material concerns

Though still dependent upon that with the word as we are users of these syllables
threading among us fleshy sentences

6.

the barista's skin was golden as she exposed her lower back while bending.
I appreciate it but
must move on since

—the chives are growing in this spring—like spiked and greased locks on a punker's head

and the tabby cat stares at me from the driveway where that car's parked whose hubcap I retrieved last month and gave to the neighbor, my hands filthy as a result of my charity

---

10. "In the beginning was the word, and the word was with God, and God was the word." John 1:1 (translation mine)

so must remain in the chapping wind as I hope to avoid more cracking
threads near the nails

—which would not heal until ". . . Aprill with his shoures soote"[11] (now
passed) so fingers
   sealed

and healed of the woes of winter and its lingering aftermath, swinging at
the ends of arms as they help propel me up the hill to home where rest lies
after the season's sweat dries

in the welcome air leaving me, after a portion of hour,
in my own skin, light and still as only welcome fatigue can leave me

7.

in the warm these days,
I have nothing of which to complain

leftovers make a fine meal for lunch,
which should only be casual, after all,

last night's salmon upon a bed of two-day-old
bulgur wheat, no extra expense
to tax a budget with unnecessary cost,
even though every day is a special occasion

but one that does not demand a special outlay
to maintain its status, which we should
remember as if the quotidian is merely
one as any other

---

11. Geoffrey Chaucer, *The Canterbury Tales* 1.1

8.

My dreams pass through the gates of ivory,
whose smooth sides must provide ease
for fantasy whose lineaments

melt like neglected ice cream in the warm
light of waking, whose heat insists
upon the solidity of the real,

brooking no sinuous semi-solids
to opiate the atmosphere, whose
idol is the only sun, a brazen

master directing all to duty and task,
the no-nonsense of the now
sating one's time

in to-do's and while one has time
that will yield again to slack
vision behind closed eyes

9.

So the engine drives me onward,
        a wheel of adamantine spinning within my cell(f)
not like that of Ixion but vehement nonetheless

until the final stop after revolutions uncountable
        at least to our limited means to grasp destiny
Fortuna ultimately allots so leaving us with only

the flame of inspiration as guide through a life
        of acquisition and discarding what is not needed
just dropped as dross without regret or thought

Twenty-Four in Twenty-Four

Cracks *(6-7 a.m.)*

The day cracks upon me, leaving only
my conscious mind to reap the cold harvest
of early morning, dark in the fall, denatured
I muse but just slightly for I do not
like to think in the minutes after the
alarm gushes its grate to my once graced
ears, now pierced by the hellish repeating
screek, accompanied by the satanic
red that squares out the nether time when I
must mannequin myself into upright
obedience and push my unwilling
self to start the already shattered day
but to stumble is to walk and that is
better than not at all so I'll take the scrape.

Igniting Solace *(7-8 a.m.)*

Warm water, clothes, caffeine, and sustenance
have mended the rift spread by that tenebrous
starting dell from which I rose at a start
so the plastic cement of moving forward
gives me stability in the clean light
that hones the rising sky to cutting edge
on which my careful eyes rest soft, unharmed
and even flourish as they imbibe blue
extract igniting solace from what was
once cold coal or maybe gray slate veined with
only ice for the instantly cold when
that summons arrived a blank span ago
so black back then but far gone now as I
just keep moving into the curling minutes.

Business Smacks *(8-9 a.m.)*

The hard business smacks but in certain grade light
at least my eyes are open and can defend
against any onslaught that will only be a flitch
of the initial shock and then quicken into
further smoothing as it moves along, but
in this hour the colors sharpen even
those destined for only useful marking
of substance, which will never rise above
that solid, stolid thingness as it squats
on whatever space it needs for its time
and I hope to just ease into those shades
imagine I am useful like the frogged object
if I can fill a need and feel freed from
the glum before, I can crank this through to next.

Facility Refined *(9-10 a.m.)*

No excuse or even real weight drags
upon me in this slot of ripening
time where life has become mechanical
but not sterile, just humming along in
a smooth honey flow permeating life
to those awake in this crisp cut destined
for duties inspired or otherwise
connecting the cog in a chain to ends
or gliding the wing or puffing the leaf
toward the ground of faded comfort down
after this supple striding on land with
facility refined in going grace
that provides push, the smacking apex of
activity from where we may leap to great.

Stride Slackens *(10-11 a.m.)*

The humming machine satisfied in its
stride slackens, not with fatigue or despair
but only because the scent of noon joy
rides yet subtle in this hour whereby
the growing proximity to twelve hours
in light banishes the phantom of morn
to non-existent till the next rising
so amble even in my stride and use
the inertia earned from times devoted
to working and thinking and a bit of
unctuous dreaming, putting minds semi-
sated in oases under palm fronds' blades
now cruise, reclining slightly, eyes on goal
though my up time is only less than half gone.

Coast or Lean *(11 a.m.-12 p.m.)*

Now I must admit that we coast or lean
into that gradual descent to noon
where lies the island of plenty for just
a luxurious slice zesting between
beginning and continuation, flat
as the horizon stretching without care
into desired infinity, space to sun
only to meet with thudding impact on
arrival, where I meet the wall against
the start-over but my imagination gets
the best of my expectations as I roll
closer to that blank stop, crease in the cloth
maintain focus I say, a manager to one
and set a course toward the gentle place.

Deem That Time Cease *(12-1 p.m.)*

The turning arrives wearing whatever
pigment it likes, flushing out remaining
flecks, meandering fluffs of morning past
and scintillating novice minutes with
post meridiem dust acknowledging
the present alternation toward
the falling into dark and cool even
if this moves toward the zenith of light,
of warmth generally and perks me just
props me as I laze for this interstice
in which we may deem that time cease and work
dissolves like the resistance of still limbs
and I crown myself monarch for a span
and my otiose dreams minister to me.

Re-Start *(1-2 p.m.)*

Returning, resigning the selfish den
reentering the skein energized but
besotted with sandwich and sun topping
albeit even on a rainy day
resigned to trek to the course's demise
that lies unseen far from the lost idle.
This re-start calls for more discipline than
I have mustered since dawn-rising, dark prime.
Is it more effective to blank the mind
or imagine the terminus waiting
like a mother's arms for the traveler's
return, certainty of perfect welcome?
The vision coruscates already in my
desire before I have determined the way.

Feather Fall *(2-3 p.m.)*

Feather fall in languid snow to the ground
as our wings sag into sad fatigue slowing
to stillness after lolling in regions
where air is easy to push in passing
but lately I arrived in this nexus
of nothing far from paradise. I stall
in the nullity of an anonymous
afternoon hour where duty expects me
to hunker down on the pedal and grind
the heavy gear to the summit of what?
How can disregarded wheels claim my spring
again I as have been beyond the yoke?
But I must contain the attempted flight
I need all of myself on the road right now.

Swelled the Stream *(3-4 p.m.)*

The rain has swelled the stream once arid and
now nudges my slackened limbs toward the
delta where I will float on the salt water
warm from the accumulated daylight
yet sweet to drink whenever I might desire,
replenishing the cells worn from the track.
Dismantle that scene, however, from my
mind I will. Just reach the end of kept time
under another's authority, shackled
to purposes other than those I deemed fit
to spend effort and attention when I
could have spun off on a lark to spaces.
Again, just sixty minutes, nothing more.
Pace the engine through to *fait accompli*—stop.

Fresh Breeze *(4-5 p.m.)*

The exodus has arrived for me
and I am no different from the rest
who saunter or scramble into the sun
even if it is only metaphor.
It is real to those reentering
unrestricted space where blossom tough blooms
resplendent with quick possibility
—Not that the locus of employment is
a prison hell—but that smack of fresh breeze
freedom is tough to beat in its moment,
relegating the stack of eight hours to
never been almost at least till next rise.
So I will savor always this release
remembering the reverberation of if.

Certainly Not Idle *(5-6 p.m.)*

Latent, nascent activity erupts
my own directed energy toward
a private goal important only to
my sense of achievement. Yes, a kingdom
but certainly not idle, for it is
the center of exertion, expression
a happy storm for myself alone
a summit before the slow descent to
evening concerns soft in the setting sun.
As this interval will see those heights of
recreation it will feel right to sink
into those coming landings in the dim,
but now I will work on myself—punch my
own clock—the effort will yield my own gain.

Table *(6-7 p.m.)*

The table becomes the nexus for more than
nourishment of tired flesh fat and bones—
but the knot of knowledge passing from one
to another, the consolidation
of day's labor and emotion, tying
up threads into strong woof and warp, making
the fashioned cloth whole patterns precisely
to our liking, the only hands upon
it ours, secure within walls and warmth we
converse, construct until the tapestry
unfurls, flies in the air of dusk, dark or
not. It does not matter in what season,
for wine and dinner designate their own.
Let us celebrate we have won the day.

Separate but Amicably *(7-8 p.m.)*

We separate but amicably, one
upstairs, one downstairs, to pursue our mind's
delights within our oasis of light,
though muted, to harmonize with the dark
inking the outside world. Even this night
during the work week seems to offer much
beyond the possibilities of day
constrained by occupation, though really
just four hours stretch between now and sleeping,
precious span for reading, writing, playing—
whatever my mind desires before I
must rest, drop every shred of mental work,
since my conscious must drop for a deep spell
I will work hard to invoke the Muses' gift.

Coursing *(8-9 p.m.)*

Inspiration drowns the minutes. Constant
wash of art, language, and thought coursing through
brainways at flood stage, depositing silt
rich in fertilizing agents; future
vegetation rising from the new earth
I have created in these planting spans
with roots reaching to profundity where
lies the wisdom of the ancient world, which
upon my delving will yield seed for my
own art in today's and the near morrow's
light and atmosphere, wherein I must walk
at times while leaving this soil fallow,
all the more reason to cultivate this time
and trust the inactivity to bear fruit.

Must Slow *(9-10 p.m.)*

The mind must slow, tired after quadruple
effort: work, exercise, scholarship, and
art. Yet I would rather feel spent in the
brain than empty, sated on images
sent from afar, meant to sell unneeded
product to fatten corporate paunches
already obese on luxuries, theirs
and others', when we really need quiet
discipline to know what we need and what
to discard. Later I will relent and
yield to the slack tide already creeping
into every fiber of my knowing.
So finish I will but not before I
Have created or taken in something new.

Unwind *(10-11 p.m.)*

Yet all must unwind and eventually
stop, so before I cease all for the day
I fathom my guitar till brain and arm
loosen, drop pick and fingers, put away
the instrument, to soak in the easy
melisma of the television's drone song
thrumming the semi-dark, which I prefer
at this time, as the interior should
mimic the exterior, and the shade
on the lamp makes the light reminiscent
of fire from a long-gone age and frees my
mind to drift even in, but beyond, the
blue-white almost late night catatonic
mill that will grind to mush if I don't reach, still.

Still Yields *(11 p.m.-12 a.m.)*

Squeezing the day to its dregs, though nothing
so worthless actually, as it yields
liquor worth the effort even as strength fades
as minutes progress toward the new end,
and though I would like to meet that turning,
awake, I discipline myself to give
up near the middle of this last hour.
Weekends will find me greeting and moving past
into the sparse ever novel numbers
where I believe my imagination
will discover the needed seed for the next
crop, whenever it may burst above ground.
So consolation lies currently in
the terminal push as far as I can go.

Silent Originary *(12-1 a.m.)*

Unconscious the beginning often finds
me during the five-day stretch when I must
retire earlier than my wont, but times
do find me aware for a spell in that
silent originary, obeying
body's needs or mind's anxieties for
a snap, but the motivation is too
strong, the initial urge to sleep precludes
lengthy waking now in the unknown dark
though dreaming is shallow at this surface
scratch of slumber. The miner has delved
only feet into the rich lode lying
beneath. So I will take the urge to rise
sometimes. For it will pass and let me dig deep.

First Far Down *(1-2 a.m.)*

Now I descend deep into my own earth
and can hardly recollect the rare finds
so I must construct an artifice in words
of this first far down residence for the
easy night into which I have settled, heavy
as death but not so lengthy as that end.
In this sunken footing, nether worms must
push their segments and seams from the unseen
to the dream seen to undulate in thick
strata before my sanded eyes blind to
any light lunar or otherwise up
in real space whither I will return.
But now I have dropped to the bottom web,
groping, tangled, mazed in phantoms of seem.

Cut Loose *(2-3 a.m.)*

The precedent is profound, so the mind
must wander without an anchoring edge
throughout the boundless, without conscious guide,
cut loose, delved desert down. Only rarely
do I break to day-understanding, but
not willingly, for the forgetting is
welcome, a cleansing passed without desire
of witness, a just doing, vital for
the upright hemisphere where I must walk
too soon aware and responsible to
the law of know and comprehend. No, this
nadir is necessary ignorance,
whence I will crescent, arrive at waking
surface tension, up fathoms far from the drop.

Ocean Wide *(3-4 a.m.)*

No longer the mining metaphor, it's
too vast for knowable mineral walls.
The tunnel has flooded into ocean wide,
teeming with teasing trilobites of odd,
in the mutable Morphean wash
where glides a killer, to rip the swimmer
from the womb of not really, where he
is lolling, cleansing wounds, restoring shine
worn from waking—then swift as an alarm
I'm snatched to the sharp air and gasp with gills,
yearning for a plunging current to sweep
me down and along the submarine stream
But I lie now arid, aching awake
and pray the shark releases me to dark down.

Final Forget *(4-5 a.m.)*

And with the luck of physiology
or fortune I descend again, slackened
into the trench for a final forget
in the absolute deep, absent, blithely
absolved from all notions of care and call
carousing among coral caverns, span
lost in unreckoning ways, never to
be traced by divers, satellite-led.
I, but not I, knowing, redound in rest,
spun in currents, spinning in turn on my
own motive power around the axis
of ought even speeding up to whirling
before I must unbeknown to me
begin the rough return to the surface stress.

Breaks *(5-6 a.m.)*

Creaks—pops, the seal breaks, and the ocean spills
into nothing, the swimmer rises on
the rush toward the serrated cusp
that awaits the drifter, in the next slice, not
welcome, for the natator wishes to push
without effort into infinite ways,
sightless twines of soft crystal, safe in the
gentle dark. Yet even in the draining wake
once, twice, thrice, I slip down into the silent
source, drinking for the last from ancient stores
that in drops will cling when the clang arrives,
marking the renewal of the cycle.
So now I relish the last shards of sleep
until I must ascend from that lasting deep.

www.ingramcontent.com/pod-product-compliance
Lightning Source LLC
Chambersburg PA
CBHW061251040426
42444CB00010B/2345